DE-NIGERIANIZATION

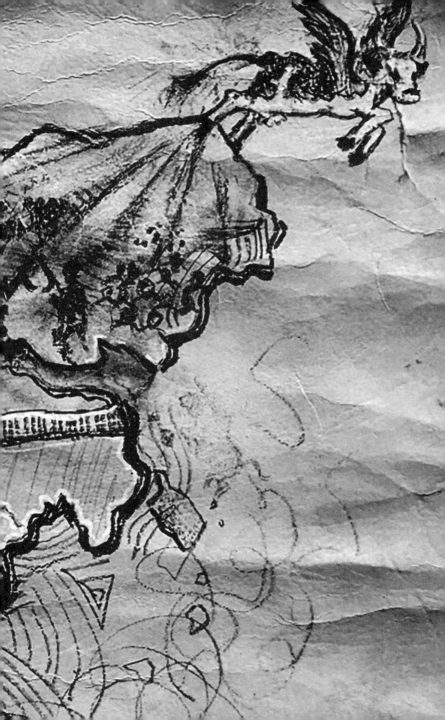

DE-NIGERIANIZATION

THE IMPERATIVE
OF RECONDITIONING

RAPHAEL ADEBAYO

New York & London

First published in Great Britain in 2022 by Abibiman Publishing

www.abibimanpublishing.com

Copyright © 2022 by Raphael Adebayo

Abibiman Publishing is registered under Hudics LLC in the United States and in the United Kingdom.

ISBN: 978-1-9989958-5-1

Cover design by Gabriel Ogunbade

Printed in the United Kingdom by Clays Ltd.

PREFACE

This book is a short read. The goal at this moment is not to deliver a ponderous work but to highlight the foundational and crystallizing issues which make the Nigerian contraption an out-and-out contrivance of despoliation and subjugation. It is a paraenesis for untainted reasoning, a desideratum for collective consciousness, an awakening to necessity, and an emphatic call to action. The reader will find in it the author's justification for the termination of sixty years of brazen rapine and inverted consociation.

EPIGRAPH

We hold these truths to be self-evident, that all men are created equal, that they are endowed by their Creator with certain unalienable rights, that among these are Life, Liberty and the Pursuit of Happiness. That to secure these rights, governments are instituted among men, deriving their just powers from the consent of the governed; that whenever any form of government becomes destructive of these ends, it is the right of the people to alter or to abolish it, and to institute new government, laying its foundation on such principles and organising its powers in such form, as to them shall seem most likely to effect their safety and happiness.

—Declaration of Independence, July 4, 1776.

CONTENTS

rative hence could become tenuous without proper
acknowledgement of its inherent multiplicity. And
you were hindered by the more casual forms of

1

FUNDAMENTALS

The multiplicity of reality often carries with it a powerful instruction for the mind to intuit and deconstruct. Reality, being a construct of one's observations and experiences, or a material condition—physical or abstract, terrestrial or spiritual—at any given time, is also contingent on the constant metamorphosis of thought and the intricacy of context. Our capacity to appreciate reality, hence, could become tenuous without proper acknowledgement of its inherent multiplicity. And yet, we are burdened by the instructional force of this phenomenon to the extent that proportionate action is the only befitting response. To understand this is to understand the force behind the following 'fundamentals' and avowals.

Nigeria is a concrete dystopic tragedy. Indeed this dystopia is too real to be situated in abstraction: it is too unwieldy to ever work, too bloodied to ever heal, too undone to veritably be. No amount of patching—which has been the country's material reality since formation—can save it from the black hole for which it is destined. The ordinary people within its geographical space, surely, are made for better fortunes only when Nigeria as presently configured and known has vanished completely. For an entity to be worthy of an unshaken place in ontic space, it must be founded on a ground that supports collective prosperity. Nigeria fails this test of first principles.

The elite-contrived reverie for Nigerians as a destined collective with a manifest destiny is fallacious: it lacks the cardinal elements of a nation and so cannot materialize. This country is founded on deceit, greed and injustice and has dwelt on wobbly feet ever since. No existential question like Nigeria can be answered flippantly, forcibly or in a rudderless fashion. That the country, in its present material condition, is to some an element of hopeful consideration is a puerile wish that can neither be justified nor objectified by any stretch of the imagination. Remove the very few suckling the milky teat of the Nigerian treasury, and their sinecures and lickspittles benefitting from the drooping crumbs and you will see the obvious fallacy of unity or collective prosperity. You will find the compelling apologue of a fox in the hen-house where the one regards the others as nothing but game.

The pervasive inclination towards avarice and superfluous accumulation to the detriment of the majority, mainly in political stratosphere from which all else cascades, is largely evocative of the depraved value-system inherited at state formation. In other words, George Goldie and Frederick Lugard birthed a lie and a vesication on the day of Amalgamation. The 1914 amalgam not only devalued the collective and the individual, but it also continues to perpetuate value-decay and render injustice supreme. It was this carbuncle of avaricious inclination that motivated the canalization of the 1962 and 1963 census fraud—incensed by the inveterate North-South cynicism, an invidious British predilection towards the North and its ill-founded trepidation of communist apparition in the ideological orientation of the erudite south—through a rather narrow tunnel of statecraft as a united entity, though of contradictory forces and nationalities. Ahmadu Bello—himself an inveterate ethno-nationalist and a 'Northerner first' champion—

once avowed what is common knowledge but must be reiterated that before amalgamation, *'...there was no country called Nigeria. What is now Nigeria consisted of a number of large and small communities all of which were different in their outlooks and beliefs... and these many and varied communities have not knit themselves into a composite unit.'*[1] The only omission in this otherwise truthful statement is that some of those communities are more agreeable and forward-looking, by way of ethnological gravitation, than the others and will do well together without the perfervid feudal overlords among them. Hence, in his more succinct affirmation, Bello declared: *'The mistake of 1914 has come to light, and I should like it to go no further.'*[2] No doubt, this should become the sole refrain of the South and Middle-Belt in Nigeria.

No type of patching or fiat can impel organic patriotism in Nigeria, in the same way it is immanent for the British or Russian. Occasionally, no doubt, there will be the *Stephen A. Smith Moments*[3], when Nigerians across ethnic divisions collectively reject a condescension that bears on all; but this is only a

---

1 (Bello, 1962)

2 (Forsyth, 1969)

3 *American Sports Journalist Stephen Anthony Smith invited the ire of most Nigerians over his jaundiced denigration of the Nigerian Basketball Team, after Team USA was defeated by the Nigerian team.*

natural response to whatever is perceived by a people or community—forcibly under a shared identity or not—as a targeted insult, and does not particularly indicate internal congruity, nor organic patriotism.

Alongside its repute as the most populous country of black people on earth—a repute which continues to appear more important than its concrete reality—Nigeria is also the extreme poverty capital of the world, also one of the most corrupt countries in the world, also one of the most repressive places in the world, also one of the most insecure places to live in the world and one of the most fecund grounds for dehumanization and injustice in the world. With a population projection of over four hundred million by 2050 and a projected two hundred and sixty million by 2030, the immediate future of this contraption has not been any bleaker, and the urgency of reconditioning has never been greater.

There have been many a treatise in the past—some even now, on how to make Nigeria work as an African prototype of transformative change—but that will never happen because Nigeria was never designed to work in that sense. As a rentier construct, Nigeria was heinously designed to service the peremptory interests of the British. It is this culture of rentiership (steeped in petro-politics, etc.) that post-colonial politicians and liveried dictators became inured to, and which has cascaded down the twenty-first century military-civilian socio-political culture in a brutal fashion. No surprise, then, that the twenty-first-century Nigerian political elite is either a progeny of the Nigerian political class or a constituted malefactor made of no genius application but of the Nigerian dystopic condition.

Another reason Nigeria will never work is that it is founded on and lubricated with lies. To build anything on lies is to erect it on shoals and quicksands. The first lie Nigeria told itself was that it was a united country. Nothing, perhaps, ran more athwart to this fallacy than three key events after independence: First, the brutal suppression of the Tiv Agitations for self-government by Tafawa Balewa which led to the hideous dispatch of no fewer than 3000 Tivs by the then First Brigade army—the first punitive deployment of the military in post-independence Nigeria. Second, the series of post-independence massacres of Igbos and other Easterners which culminated in the antebellum pogrom of late 1966, leaving numerous thousands of Igbos and other Easterners—women, fetuses and children included—mangled, beheaded, despoiled, dislodged, wholly dehumanized and traumatized. Third, the conviction upon trial and imprisonment of Western politicians who heralded the country's independence barely three years into it. That case of treasonable felony and the decimation of thousands of Tivs on their native land, and the bilious carnage against the Igbos and other Easterners, indicated the future recrudescence of the country's existential disunity, which was—and still is—truer and stronger than any sham union expediently organized for independence at all cost which, in its most extreme apogee, later ushered in the uniformed Big Brothers barely six years into independence, and eventually, the so-called 'Civil War'.

The trade-offs between Northern and Southern Nigeria that culminated in an independent Nigerian state were unreasonable trade-offs for the long term. Since the dawn of post-colonial Nigeria, the social and especially political policies of the country have increasingly been a reflection of the ethnic and religious ambitions of one part of the country—the core-north[4]—over the others. Rather than foster

---

4   *The core-north are the northern parts of the Nigeria that are predominantly Hausa/Fulani and united under the Muslim faith. They are the northern States where Sharia law is both instituted and rigorously enforced. Historically these States tend to have a similar voting pattern. And their votes predominantly goes to political candidates that represents their religious aspirations and speak to their ethno-cultural anxieties. (See figure 1 for a map of Nigeria's core-north.)*

ethnic unity, this section obstinately continues to merchandise its contorted idea of political superiority and numinous domination over other nationalities. The core-north essentializes Nigeria's unseemliness as an unworkable contraption. The age-long supposition that Nigeria's unity can be perfunctorily engineered or by and by commandeered is a historical fallacy rooted in both naivete and sheer villainy.

By no commonsensical yardstick was it appropriate for that region of northern Nigeria, rooted in the subjugator predilection of Usman dan Fodio, whose sense of good living was in the imperialistic domination of all else, to which the other tribes in the other territories within that region of present Nigeria—several scores of them, Tiv and Jukun included—were impelled tributaries who considerably remained so even after amalgamation, to be included in a closely knit 'one nation' basket, wherein it was only ever going to constitute a dialectical contradiction. The assumption hence, that both sides of the hemisphere are one and the same was wrong then and remains so now. We may call it a perennial clash of value systems.

Independence—true independence from Britain—would have been to revert to pre-colonial geographical structures wherein the south and the north enjoyed the liberty to embrace their respective socio-cultural, religious and political value systems. The intractable recrudescence of socio-cultural variances which, par for the course, succeeded the pre-independence forfeit of that very element on the altar of political expediency, continues to fervidly calcify agitations for the severance of other conscious nationalities. It is hence, no staggering peculiarity that of all the regions in the Nigerian contraption, only the core-northern region retains such dehumanizing spaces as a '*Strangers' Colony*,' commonly known as '*Sabon Gari*'—mostly inhabited by southern and middle-belt nationalities, or non-Hausa-Fulani nationalities—in spite of its rather stupefyingly audacious averment of unity. The lies that hoodwinked southern architects of post-independence Nigeria to suppose a fallacious unity, abandoning history and logic for expediency, are continuously exposed by perennial existential scrimmages and secessionist agitations, fecundated by the ever-growing realization of Nigeria's material incongruities.

Southern Nigeria, in point of fact, historically recorded its most encouraging advancement in contemporary human and economic innovation between the late forties and the fifties. From the East to Western Nigeria, there was appreciable human development and societal advancement in the south.

There was also a very huge education chasm between the north and the south. Expectedly, education and other forms of social development deepened the existing socio-cultural gulf between both regions, and this has considerably remained so till this day, quota system or not. The want of logic, innovation and human-centred development in governance is a direct consequence of the pollution of stations of authority with backward-minded elements; but to perpetuate the suckling of this country's treasury by advantaged elements, what should be is wilfully immolated by the political elite for what should not.

Further, the embedded culture of impunity in the Nigerian contraption is another reason it can never work. Here, the main issue is not malfeasance, which is arguably human nature, but cultural impunity, which lubricates and hurtles malfeasance towards cataclysmic levels. Impunity is malleable and beatable, but cultural impunity is not—in that it normalizes impunity and rewards it unabashedly. It is cultural impunity that emboldens the subhuman butchery of peaceful protesters and the imputing of monkeys and snakes for mindless defalcation.

Whether it is a State Governor caught on camera stuffing hillocks of slush funds into his rather commodious pockets, or a former president who looted $8 Billion to found a steel foundry that never produced a single bar of steel, or a brutal dictator's offshore transfer of unquantifiable amounts of looted capital, cultural impunity merely absolves criminals of repercussions and often, it grants them meritorious awards to boot. Nigeria cannot, therefore, reform its way out of cultural impunity. It is extensively systemic and osmotically ingrained into the brains of its political elite. It is too grounded that its very existence is cast in stone.

Light years have passed, and cultural impunity has become a common denominator—from the highest stations of authority to the venal machines of state bureaucracies, otherwise called the civil service—in the Nigerian contraption, and it continues to sink deeper into society. Its currency as a detail of the Nigerian contraption is repulsively extensive. In wretched situations like this, only a radical reconditioning can make a difference.

Equally, one is fain to note that some might say that these penumbrae of chronic nodi are insufficient to make such assertions as aforementioned, that these are mere platitudes of age-long familiarity. But, we must note that it is exactly this pattern of subtilising dysfunctionality as a concomitant of state-building that has now kept the country at hell's gate.

When hallucination ravages the mind to the extent of delirium—in the same way that it does the crusaders of this misbegotten contraption—the fallacy of hope becomes more fantastic than concrete reality itself. There are, au fond, two divisions by which the Nigerian tragedy may be characterized: the ordinary people's fatalism on the one hand, and the inveterate character of the country's dysfunctionality as personified by the political class on the other.

For the latter, it is essentially true that the incapacity of the political class for transformative actions, and the fatuous assumption by the southern wing of this class that the country will magically stumble into better fortunes, accentuates the delirium through which it hopes to perpetuate this contraption. By the same token, this political class remains oblivious to the mounting human cost that their boneheaded fantasy begets. For the former, however, the situation is different but no less sad. At issue is the ossified culture of dehumanization which inevitably induces material and psychological poverty. Both are not mutually exclusive; but psychological poverty, many a time, degenerates into fatalism—which could be of any type; but often political, along with a sense of despondency—and sometimes sycophancy. Lack of material comfort, however, compromises one's capacity to act in their own best interest or at the very least, not to act against it.

In the final analysis, it must be emphasized that Nigeria has simply failed to answer the numerous existential questions of its people and, in consequence, is unworthy of perpetuation. The ceaseless gripe of the Nigerian masses has now reached the point where a particular sense of praxis is required to strip the veil dissembling the Nigerian contraption. The question, therefore, is not whether or not Nigeria deserves 'Nigerians'—because it doesn't. The real question is: for how long can 'Nigerians' endure Nigeria?

Figure 1. Map of Nigeria's Core-North

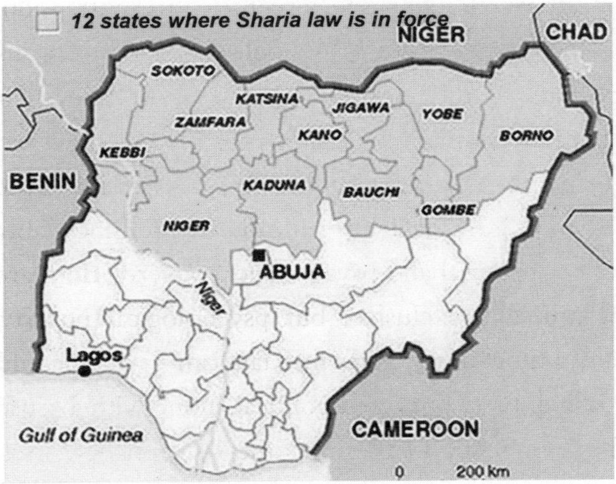

Source: Mmoh, 2020

2

THE NORTHERN PROBLEM

In the vast world of contraries, one pernicious contradiction which, among others, must be swiftly confronted in Nigeria is that of the region known as Northern Nigeria. By this, I specifically refer to the core-north or the twelve sharia-compliant states.[5] Inflated with imperial pride courtesy of Britain's bias and the canker of 1914, the core-north's idea of an independent Nigeria is one in which it superimposes its wishes on the other nationalities. A Nigeria where it exercises suzerainty over all

5   *Sharia states: Zamfara State, Kano State, Niger State, Bauchi State, Sokoto State, Katsina State, Borno State, Jigawa State, Kebbi State, Yobe State, Kaduna State, Gombe State.*

other nationalities in the country. Its vision of post-colonial Nigeria is the vision of its conquistadors of the nineteenth century. Its idea of a united Nigeria is one in which it contributes the least, takes the most, and demands absolute fealty from other nationalities. It is this contrived sense of its own worth and purpose in the Nigerian contraption, that has exacerbated the country's material reality as a world of two irreconcilable opposites.

At the surface, there appears to be nothing necessarily wrong with anyone from the core-north and the *talakawa*—plebians, who, like millions of others in the south, are victims of economic deprivations by Nigeria's bourgeois capitalists and political elite. But between this *talakawa* class of core-northerners and those between them and their blue-blooded rulers, there is tacit complicity for the core-north's imperial ambitions: the overwhelming majority of the ordinary core-northerner, literate or analphabetic, do not antagonize their leaders' pernicious imperial schemes on the strength of its antagonism to Nigeria's claim to unity. When, for instance, in late 1999 the erstwhile governor of Zamfara State, Ahmed Sani Yerima, proclaimed that his state would adopt Sharia in the first month of the following year, he was adorned with northern ballads by both the commoners and the core-north's political elite who had found the deus ex machina to their misrule, and soon followed Zamfara's path until all twelve core-northern states became fully Sharianized. The fact that it happened under President Olusegun Obasanjo, a Christian from southern Nigeria was an unexceptionable attestation of feudalistic disdain and ambition. Never mind the said president's charlatanry of confronting the wild beast with bare hands, or as may also be argued— running with the hare and hunting with the hounds. No argument then, as is the case now, would override the compelling contradiction of Sharia's adoption in the core-north, and the facile claim to Nigeria's unity by force, by the same lot. As the Shia fundamentalist, Ibrahim El Zakzaky, correctly precised it then: *'Islamic law is meant to be applied by an Islamic government in an Islamic environment. If you introduce Islamic laws under an un-Islamic environment, under a system of government which is not Islamic, then it is bound to be an instrument of oppression.'* [6] At any rate one Buba Jangebe had his right hand lopped off, in line with a Sharia court's verdict in Zamfara State, for rustling a cow. His response to losing a hand is 'I thank God for the amputation.'

More recently, in late 2020, one Yahaya Sheriff

---

6   (Maier, 2002)

was sentenced to death by hanging in Kano State by a Sharia court—for allegedly committing blasphemy against the idolized begetter of Islam, Muhammad— on WhatsApp. The most prominent core-northerners either withheld commentary on the issue or unstintingly expressed support. The point here is not to pillory this aspect of Islam (which should typically command more space than the present work allows) but to highlight the inherent contradictions of the Nigerian state. It is to depict the hierarchical standings of citizens inhabiting the same geographical sphere but never afforded the same rights; for there are other non-Muslim individuals and ethnic groups in northern Nigeria whose lives are existentially impinged on due to this very contradiction: a theocratic State Government operating within a purportedly secular Federation. At the centre of the Sharia issue, however, is a clear variance to be found in a portion of Nigeria's constitution which claims that 'the Government of the Federation or of a state shall not adopt any religion as state religion.' But in its neon-lit eminence, Sharia is less an antagonism of the constitution's lyrical flummery; and more importantly, the majority of core-northerners deem it so.

By declaring its region Sharia-compliant, the

core-north instantiated its collective idée fixe for domination through Islamization and laid the bricks for future forms of core-northern expressions for imperial domination—Boko Haram, Fulani herders/militia, Miyetti Allah (both Kautal Hore and MACBAN), etcetera etcetera—a curiously veridical sequel to the rump of Yan Tatsine and indeed, the 1804 Jihadists. For fear of objurgation and perhaps losing access to the slush funds and political support from the core-north, those who should confront this horrendous reality merely recoiled—and still do. But it has always been there in our faces—that one could draw a straight line between Boko Haram and the Sharianization agenda that emanated from Zamfara State in 1999 under Governor Ahmed Sani Yerima.

Here, we must emphasize that more than a mere symbol of analogous remanences, there is an emphatic exactitude between the administrative modus operandi of Boko Haram today, particularly in regard to its imposed imposts on residents of its conquered territories in Northern Nigeria, which was the exact model through which Usman dan Fodio and later his son, Muhammadu Bello, expanded and entrenched the suzerainty of the Sokoto Jihad Caliphate across a broad sweep of emirates, provinces, and various neighbouring territories in today's Northern Nigeria in the nineteenth century. The Ribat, as it was known, 'was a fortress… [which the caliphate used] to secure the boundaries between Dar al-Islam (the land of Islam) and Dar al-Harb (the land of war) or Dar al-Kufr (the land of non-believers).'[7] Boko Haram, in effect, bears the apodictic charactery of the caliphate's Ribat Strategy—through its ruthless fundamentalist and expansionist terrorism—which makes today's Dal al-Harb or Dar al-Kufr of the core-north in general easily discernible to uncluttered eyes.

The vicious campaign of wilful invasions of peaceful communities in the north, often Christian-dominated, by Fulani herders and other unidentified ethnonationalist elements demands studied scrutiny. This campaign of ethnoreligious culling has, over the years, dilated to the south where its extent of viciousness has stoked secessionist flames. Naturally, a united country would unanimously condemn such devilry and mobilize to swiftly pulverize it. But the Muhammadu Buhari regime, being the emblematic manifestation of core-northern commitment to Usman dan Fodio's imperial injunction, subsequently personified by his descendant Ahmadu Bello—whose private army 'Sardauna Brigade,' led the 'Igbo Must

---

7   *A History of Nigeria* by *Toyin Falola* and *Matthew M. Heaton.*

Go' violent crusade that followed the controversial 1962-63 census—has merely pussyfooted around the issue.

To be sure, Nigeria is witnessing a methodical campaign of sanguinary invasions of farmlands in the country's middle-belt and southern regions, unabated rape of women and girls, and the unlawful occupation of indigenous lands by Fulani herdsmen.[8] The implicit augury of this campaign is of no little significance and, indeed, there are two possibilities: The Fulani herders, Boko Haram terrorists and other active elements of ghoulish proclivities from the core-north, are either a conveyor belt for a tendentious imperial agenda—for which the Buhari personage is more than a capable accomplice—or as the incumbent president of Nigeria, Buhari intends to weaponize the active insurgency to perpetuate himself in power. Both possibilities are deleterious and unwise to brush aside. I have written about the latter elsewhere[9], but as for the former the possibility is even stronger. In any case, both are not mutually exclusive. One thing is for sure:

---

8   *The Global Terrorism Index declared the Fulani Herdsmen from the core-north as the fourth deadliest terrorist group in the world in 2015. The ethno-religious carnage of the terrorist group has since escalated and metastasized to southern Nigeria.*

9   *Author's piece on SaharaReporters titled Nigerians Should Prepare for Another Military Regime. May 2021.*

Gone are the days when one of our independence harbingers, Chief Awolowo, found currency in the expression that 'a disintegrated Nigeria could only consist of internecine armed camps', for temporal advantage has proven that it is the exact opposite which makes the fact inevitable.

There is an indisputable decibel of taciturnity or coherency as the case may be, among core-northerners which, to the unvarnished mind, is rather frightful. The comminatory campaign described above demands utmost attention for several reasons. There is no majority reprobation or push back from the core-north to decisively crush these depredations ravaging other nationalities of Nigeria. Contrariwise, there is now an absurdity accumulating currency, most disreputably spearheaded by Ahmad Gumi[10], that the odious brigandage of extortioners and executioners from the core-north, infamously known for their wanton kidnapping and displacement of Nigerians, is somehow deserving of clemency. Yet, as deficient in rationality as that absurdity is, there is no visible rejection of it from the core-north, not even from the supposedly 'progressive' Arewa voices on social media

---

10 *Islamic cleric from Kano State. His father, Abubakar Mahmud Gumi(1922—92), an associate of Ahmadu Bello, was a most notable proselytizer of Islamization in Northern Nigeria.*

and other conventional mediums. Perhaps their voices are louder in silence.

At any rate, clemency will no longer be about the elements of brigandage from the core-north who are mushrooming by the day, but also a movement for the extension of clemency to Boko Haram and Fulani herders. There is, in fact, a 'reintegration' scheme for 'repentant' Boko Haram terrorists.[11] It is, therefore, not far-fetched that the ultimate goal for core-northerners would be to demand clemency, with such ferocity as was done for Sharia, for Boko Haram and Fulani herders. It might, in fact, not have to demand clemency for killer herders because Buhari, as the manifestation of core-north's imperial agenda, has obstinately refused to proscribe and pulverize the murderous herders, in the same way he did peaceful self-determination movements in the south. As a veneer for pernicious schemes, these agents of depredations are quite speciously masked as peaceable nomads. And in no distant time from

---

11 *Operation Safe Corridor (OSC). An amnesty program designed to force defection from 'repentant' terrorists who surrender on their own accord. It began 2016 and has been kept in place despite its absurdity. The big question is whether it is legally permissible to grant amnesty to an individual who has yet to be tried or convicted of a crime? Or if an issue pertaining to the punishing or pardoning of terrorists/terrorism should be left for the courts or to soldiers?*

now, there may arise the imperative to revisit the crimes of these murderous herders, and the narrative of core-northerners then would be the absurdity we are hearing presently: that the murderous herders are legitimate cattlemen who only had a few skirmishes with farmers. The narrative, then, would be nothing about how many farms were destroyed, or how many villages were pillaged or violently colonized or the numerous bumptious admonishments by MACBAN, or the women raped, people rendered homeless, or civilian lives wasted. The entire carnage would simply be vindicated as proportionate violence or inexorable self-defence.

We must, therefore, confront the objective reality that the core-north will never stop demanding and destroying until the accomplishment of its imperial ambitions. By then, it would be too late for other nationalities to defend themselves or withdraw from or end the Nigerian contraption. By then, the overwhelming majority of core-northerners, including our 'progressive' friends on that side who are visibly reticent now, would have become inadvertent victims of circumstances. By then, the visible objectifications of imperial ambitions from the core-north—from the older generations alive like Buhari, Tanko Yakasai, Nasir El-Rufai, etcetera to the younger generation, most vociferously personified by Adamu Garba, Shettima Yerima, etcetera—would have become heroes of core-northern imperialism. By then, it would be too late for southerners and middle-beltans to jeremiad today's carnage and mushrooming absurdities or organize as a cohesive bloc to save their necks. By then, fundamentalist Islam and feudalism would have won.

3

ON IPOB AND ESN

On 30 May 2016, about one thousand women, men and children peacefully marching to commemorate the killing of roughly two million Biafrans between 1967-1970 by the Nigerian State were on the receiving end of a terrible, inhumane terrorist blitzkrieg by the Nigerian police and army. That murderous intervention was sanctioned by Nigeria's president and Commander-in-Chief of the Federal Armed Forces, General Muhammadu Buhari.

On that day and the day before it, a report by Amnesty International confirmed that no less than sixty of those peaceful Biafran commemorators were shot and killed, and at least seventy of them injured as a result of the attacks on those two days alone. [12] Among those who died, the report narrates, was a man who had phoned his wife minutes before the bullet lodged in his abdomen was followed by even more pellets. Bullets paid for by his taxes. His wife was still on the phone when the Nigerian army brutally dispatched him. Six others in that army truck were extrajudicially murdered. The 2016 report by Amnesty International estimates that at least one hundred and fifty pro-Biafra activists were slaughtered by Nigerian security forces between August 2015 and August 2016. [13]

To understand the weight of that massacre, we can take a quick look at England and Wales—where the number of fatal shootings during contact with the police between 2007 and 2018 was twenty-eight in all. [14] That's roughly six times below the number of Biafran activists killed by Nigerian security forces in two years, simply for commemorating those that the Nigerian state has refused to remember. Equally worthy of note are the events of Operation Python Dance II in September 2017. A senseless joint raid by the Nigerian army and police, which descended

---

12 (Amnesty International , 2016)
13 Ibid.
14 (Independent Office for Police Conduct , 2018)

upon the palace of the traditional ruler of Afaraukwu, Eze Israel Kanu—also Nnamdi Kanu's father, killed five people and injured about thirty to boot. Those who have not forgotten the video clips that emerged on the internet from that incident would recall how dishevelled the military and police left the place, allegedly in search of Kanu, who would later lose his mother to the shock she suffered from that invasion. At the time, the Indigenous People of Biafra was simply a non-violent self-determination group with a leader perceived by many as a demagogue. Yet, their only weapon at the time was protest marches, carrying with them the flag of the defunct Biafra.

Again to understand the weight of that incident, let's return to the UK where Nicola Sturgeon, First Minister of Scotland, had told British Prime Minister Boris Johnson that another referendum on Scotland's secession from the United Kingdom is a matter of 'when—not if.' Nobody—neither Britain's Prime Minister nor Queen Elizabeth II—had ordered the invasion of her home or the traumatization of her parents. That is a society where reprobates are not in positions of authority as they are in Nigeria. When Buhari exhausted his list of fabrications for the deliberate killings and human rights violations of IPOB members, he then went berserk and proscribed the group, designating it a terrorist organization whilst at the same time, more or less patting the actual terrorists—Fulani herders on the back as 'bandits' who deserve clemency, rehabilitation and reintegration into society. Even more horrendous was a speech in the aftermath of the Agatu Massacre in Benue State in which Fulani herder militia pillaged villages and left scores of Benue people dead. 'Please, accommodate your countrymen,' was Buhari's response to the communities that have refused to surrender their farmlands for grazing and 'cattle colony' by the President's tribesmen.

In the case of IPOB, one could clearly see an ethnonationalist verdict to equate terror where there was no such threat; but to hang a dog, you must first give it a bad name. The President's decision to quickly proscribe the group was a bigoted verdict to scapegoat and equate the so-far peaceful self-determination group, IPOB, with the proscription of the terrorist Boko Haram by Jonathan in 2013. No surprise, therefore, that when Pythons were dancing in the southeast, no reptile was dancing in the northwest or middle-belt where herders were raping and killing innocent civilians. This background, though non-exhaustive, is necessary for us to understand how the

Eastern Security Network, ESN[15], came to be.

According to Nnamdi Kanu, leader of the IPOB, what led to the creation of the ESN were the endless incursions of Fulani herders, the indiscriminate raping of women and the destruction of farmlands in the name of grazing in the south-east and south-south. Yet, it is indisputable that there had always been enough reasons to create an ESN as a self-defence extension of IPOB against the imperialist aggression of the Buhari regime and the core-north. [16]

The sovereignty of a state should not legitimate its wanton use of violence against its own people, except, of course, as has now become dreadfully lucid to all, the state considers those people a pariah. Peace is not a zero-sum pledge; it is a commitment that involves more than one party. Buhari has shown times without number a lack of interest in pursuing peace and conflict resolution, except when it is about his Fulani tribe. If he were, he would have followed that path instead of unprovoked violence against IPOB.

---

15 *The self-defence arm of the self-determination group, IPOB.*

16 *Add to this the perceived emasculation of South East Governors, who could not rise to the occasion to form a regional security outfit like Amotekun as done by their counterparts in the South West. Nature, as it is often said, abhors vacuum, and Kanu stepped into the void created by both the flagitious core-northern expressions spearheaded by Buhari and the inaction of the Igbo Governors.*

The emergence of the ESN became necessary the day Buhari declared war on IPOB and none on Fulani herders. The ESN is not the terrorist here—it kills no innocent civilians, even though it is perceived to have recently adopted attacks on state actors and assets as part of its strategic defiance actions. Yet, these are the fallouts of the wounds of injustice which the Buhari regime has incubated, nurtured and allowed to fester. Every action of Buhari as Nigeria's president imposes a moral responsibility of scrutiny on 'Nigerians'. Buhari has no justification for his aerial and ground raids on innocent civilians living in the south-east under the guise of ending IPOB or the ESN. No ethnic group under the bondage of the Nigerian contraption signed a contract of human rights violations and enforced disappearances, the wanton killings of protesters, and other such nefarious preoccupations of Buhari as the president of Nigeria, nay, of his ethnic group. It is an absolute travesty of justice that a group impelled to emerge for its existential survival gets proscribed as a terrorist group whilst real terrorists are cloaked in derisible identities as the state deems fit.

The Nigeria that Buhari desperately desires is one in which other nationalities are subjugated and defeated. By that token, the mediums reporting IPOB or ESN as a terrorist group are merely truckling to the terrorism of the Nigerian state. They are telling other nationalities to surrender to a terrorist and imperialist state without as much as a whimper. They are reporting injustice with the language of oppression, telling other nationalities to be weak; that defiance against oppression and injustice by an imperialist state implies terrorism. They are inadvertently suggesting that we should not be free, that freedom means being targeted and killed by the Nigerian state. But we must reject that. Freedom is scarcely an abstraction; we cannot be free and not be free.

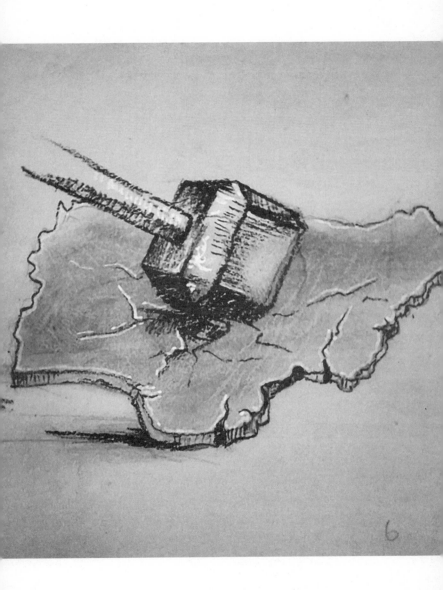

4

ON INDISSOLUBILITY

Everything is contestable—the words we write, the foods we eat, the water we drink, the privileges we claim, the smiles we see on people's faces—all of it. Nothing is socially constructed in the human world that is exempt from dialectical contestations. Every human contrivance is subject to the vicissitudes of malleability. That is why the absolutist claim that Nigeria's so-called unity is incontestable is senseless elite propaganda that lacks substance and is in fact, stupefying to the human mind. It essentially underplays the dystopic tragedy of the Nigerian contraption, a negation of the uncontainable disillusion.

The cloven hoof of this elite propaganda lies in its dubious narrative: that it was ordained by some ethereal force to which we must surrender our agency and capacity for dialectical observations. To the unvarnished mind, no case has ever been made that was compelling enough to logically convince one that the continuance of this contraption on the basis of its fictive unity is sensible. Pretending to be united might have been enough at independence, but keeping a country together certainly requires more than that. Awolowo's prediction of internecine carnage has, in fact, ravaged the Nigerian contraption more times than disintegration ever would have. If at all it ever would have. For, in sooth, partitioning Nigeria is in the best interest of all concerned.

There have been countless instances when the Nigerian contraption should have suffered absolute immolation, but three are of towering significance. The first was in 1967 when the Nigerian state launched its barbaric bloodletting on the Igbos, and the other nationalities either surrendered to somnific reasoning or resisted that war of liberation, even violently, save for a very tiny few. Consequently, the Ogoni people suffered next when Abacha hung Ken Saro-Wiwa and eight others in the most shambolic court verdict Africa has ever seen. The second time was during the June

12 struggle, when Kudirat Abiola and eventually her husband, Moshood Abiola, were brutally assassinated. The majority of the Igbos, having been mostly neglected by the other nationalities during Nigeria's war against the Igbos, exhibited only a tiny, fugacious solidary for the Ogonis after the Ogoni Nine and the Yorubas after Abiola's termination. In other words, the lack of unity among the southern and middle-belt nationalities has delayed the collapse of the Nigerian contraption till this moment.

The third time to put paid to the contraption called Nigeria is now. All southern and middle-belt nationalities—or most at least—within the Nigerian contraption are presently suffering one form or the other of wicked decimation and injustice by the core-north, whose refractoriness to accelerate its imperial ambition continues to intensify in volcanic proportions. The Fulani herders, Boko Haram and the so-called 'bandits'—all of whom are branches of the same tree—have, somehow, 'naturally' become a permanent component of the Nigerian state. It will be foolhardy for any of the other ethnic nationalities to assume that these agents of imperial belligerence will somehow, magically disappear. They are the very reification of the imperial idée fixe of the core-north.

It requires no genius to admit that the 'One

Nigeria' ship is in troubled waters. The Indigenous People of Biafra, IPOB, the Eastern Security Network, ESN, the several Niger Delta armed groups, the Oduduwa Republic, etcetera—are not mere speckles of opposing values or agitations of misguided elements—they all are the faces of the long-suppressed Nigerian condition—which should have been well-considered before the contraption was rammed down the oesophagi of all constituent nationalities. These movements and proponents of dissolution have become revenants that will not go away. But we must note that the greatest failure of Nigeria is not that it pretended to be united at independence, it is that it has continually deceived itself that it is united and has woefully failed to be united in spite of independence. To insist, however, that Nigeria's indissolubility is settled and incontestable in spite of current realities, is to embrace folly and discountenance the foreboding apocalypse.

To be sure, the problem of Nigeria's unity is a dialectical contrariety between centrifugal and centripetal forces. The political elite, for reasons rooted only in their self-gratification, are nebulously determined to defend this contraption, as agents of centripetal predilections, knowing well it will only be, as six decades have concretely proven, to the detriment of the common people. The obstinate defence of this contraption by the political elite is an obstinacy that has yet to be backed—and I am sure it never will— by such cogent reasons capable of inspiring unalloyed faith and organic patriotism. No objective mind has found any convincing rationale, as may be said of the American or British, to patriotically defend a contrived unity which, more aptly, is a figment of the elite's imagination. A King who goes about proclaiming to all and sundry that he is King is no King. Same way, the constant allusion to 'One Nigeria' does not imply Nigeria is united nor one. Rather, it is the most glaring indication that those who parrot this hollow phrase are bent on making themselves and others believe in a lie.

There is, of course, the pint-sized sect of unthinking fellows who, having been anaesthetized to agency and reasoning, would regurgitate the elite's centripetal mumbo-jumbo of unity and return to their hovels floundering in hopeless misery—a wretched state architected by the very class to which they are mere discardable weaponry. But this elitist claim of incontestable unity was ideated and now sustained without ample consideration for the benefit of the ordinary people. No genius capacity is required then, that the political class is unlikely to give up its stations of comfort and sinecurist benefits to conduce to a humanist struggle for an egalitarian society or future. Nigerian unity, therefore, is a hopeless song that its political elite must continue to sing for its own eternal thievery and jobbery.

Unlike the preternatural delusion of the political elite, there are those we may call the sublunary realists who, having rightly adjudged the Nigerian existential contradiction to be invidious and unworkable, must be prepared to prise their freedom out of this misbegotten contraption. These sublunary realists, whom we may also call *the unvarnished*—in that they vehemently hold in contempt the imperialist ambitions, stupefying reverie, mind-numbing deceit, chronic immiseration, bourgeois obsessions, inveterate venality and all forms of dehumanization, deprivation and intellectual obfuscation—which the Nigerian dystopian condition elevates so distastefully, are of such mould that they are untrammelled by the refractoriness of core-northern imperialist expressions. They are the centrifugal forces determined to ensure the freedom of southerners and middle-beltans from the Nigerian cesspool.

As for the political elite in the south and middle-belt who would rather truckle to northern imperialism than champion the much-needed liberation struggle of their people: One of the reasons for this is that Nigeria provides an incredible carapace of immunity for the so-called elected representatives to elude the people's scrutiny. They are contented being aloof from the concrete reality of their people— too contented, in fact, with delivering nothing and controlling everything, and too complicit or involved with their northern overlords to steadfastly champion the freedom, dignity and well-being of those whom they ought to serve.

The southern and middle-belt political elites who continue to avow support for Nigeria's unity have never provided any tangible conviction behind such motif. All wrangling for Nigeria's unity, therefore, is rooted purely in greed. The barbaric war against the Igbos was purely motivated by internal and external greed. The entire Nigerian bourgeois political class, through the instrumentality of their own greed are prepared to die on the hill of a malformed Nigerian state that only works for them and their coteries. The bourgeois capitalists at the top of the economic chain are also visibly motivated by greed. The journalists who formed a guild to advocate Nigeria's unity, whilst their compeers are dehumanized by the Nigerian state do so plainly for greed and lack of understanding. That is simply the objective reality.

Nigeria has betrayed its existential mandate to

unite for progressive and egalitarian development; to argue otherwise is to squander time and lives. There is no such future in which the Nigerian contraption of today would emerge from its present existential contradiction, as a truly united and generally prosperous whole.

5

THE PROBLEM OF SUPERIOR

There is a certain kind of problem with the Nigerian contraption that we may call the problem of *Superior*: this being a self-contrived imperious idea by a person or group of persons socially or politically interrelated, and influenced by a cultural, historical or subjective sense of *being* which considers the *Other* as inferior or wrong or naïve. And then, proceeds to impose that person or group of persons' idea or goal as the indisputable, even divine utility. It is an inward-looking, self-serving *weltanschauung* to concrete existence, which undergirds any form of interpersonal relations and socio-political aspirations of those afflicted by it.

In Nigeria's case, the flawed idea of Nigeria's unity is regarded as a Superior idea which we must all defend and protect, or aspire to defend and protect, irrespective of its inherent contradictions. The material reality of political dysfunction is often sidestepped with a Superior rationalization of a nascent state, ever so ridiculously propagated even after sixty years of degeneration, and in spite of the privilege of historic and contemporary civilizations. The hideously indisputable crony-capitalism—and its evil denouement of mass impoverishment and uneven society—is countered using such impossible Superior narrative of collective and sustainable development; the concrete reality of dehumanization and deprivation is often diminished using the obverse Superior narrative of political witch-hunt or subjective bias; the objective reality of all religions as a social construct railed against by religious fundamentalists with the Superior retort of impiety; the material reality of the oppressed majority exhibiting unconsciously absorbed oppressive expressions of the oppressive class, so that they become well-adjusted to their own denigration, is dismissed as infelicitous. In short, the problem of Superior can be summarized thus: that one is master and the other a vassal, that one is blind and the other is blessed with sight.

But this is at best a mystification—in itself repulsive, and at the core, an unnoticed affliction. For the Nigerian problem of Superior is a contrivance—not only in and of itself—but also of its colonial history, by which the Nigerian mind, most visibly personified through its elite or bourgeoisie, was weaned on the obverse metanarrative of the colonizer as the infallible *Superior Race,* as W.E.B. Du Bois described it—an internalization of external dehumanization and subjugation. And thus, the most deleterious colonial inheritance of Nigeria's political elite—often denied, of course—is the problem of Superior. This problem is therefore not only a 'condition' but also a 'conditioning'. The conditioning is a transient and an eradicable agent in the human. But the condition—though malleable and subject to variations—is entrenched, communicable and inheritable. The Nigerian political elites therefore, are the very embodiment of the Superior as *condition*—an affliction *sensu stricto*—which devalues the human, paralyzes his sense of consciousness and renders him a delusional object of supercilious affirmations. Suffice it to add that the ordinary Nigerian person, on account of his material reality as a personification of the oppressed class in the Nigerian contraption, can only be blighted by the *conditioning*. But the personage in the political class is mostly inextricably blighted by the *condition*.

Yet we falter if we do not go further to dualize this affliction, for indeed it exists as a dualism of the political class. And to defeat any oppressive class, we must first deconstruct it. On the one hand, there is a particular sense in which this affliction materializes more vehemently, indeed violently, in Nigeria's core-north. This is due partly to the convergence of the Superior affliction, and partly to the core-northern creed of ruthless expansionism and Islamization. There are, of course, internal and external thrusts to the northern phenomena of the Superior—but both are well-aligned to serve its historical ambition of expansionism, nurtured on Islamic fundamentalism, and diffused using the combined strength of its state and non-state actors. The internal, which is the northernization of thought, is notably ossified through its Sharia-controlled States where the core-northern agenda in 'united Nigeria' is partly settled. In those States, the fundamental components of Sharia like the public segregation of men and women, indefinite interdict on alcohol consumption (never mind that they insist on sharing in the VAT on alcohol drunk in other States), are in full force, giving credence to the aforementioned creed.[17]

The external thrust of the core-north, however, is given expression through one of its instruments of belligerency; that is, the rampaging herders—weaned on the sophistry of cattle as Superior—when, a posteriori, it is discernible to the unvarnished that expansionism and Islamization are the real Superior ambitions, being gradually canalized through the warped contraption of 'united Nigeria', into middle-belt and southern grounds. Consequently, the northern metanarrative of the Superior—the very impetus of the elite-contrived motif of 'Nigeria by force'—must be rejected through and through by middle-beltans and southerners. Never in Nigeria's contemporary history has it witnessed the current vigorous coalescence of the age-long core-northern agenda of imperialism. This may be linked to the incumbent reign of the man who probably sees himself as a Jihad 'flag-bearer', Buhari, and the culmination of an agenda that has merely been veneered in the cloak of collective nationalism for too long. The imminent

---

17 *Meanwhile, despite its interdict on Alcohol Consumption, the core-north continues to receive a huge chunk—in most cases even more than southern and middle-belt states where alcohol sale and consumption are allowed. See BusinessDay* (Ojewale, 2021)

subjugation of southern and middle-belt nationalities by the core-north—through its Superior imperial ambitions—must therefore be confronted decisively, not timidly. It is on this basis that the movement of our southern comrades—both the contemporary Biafran agitators, IPOB, and the Oduduwa Nation agitators must be commended. We must, however, as will be shown in the sequel, necessarily dilate, interweave and totalize the self-determination agitations in the south and middle-belt, in order to obviate the pitfalls of frayed agitations.

Consequently, it is equally necessary to delineate the other part of this dualism—the southern political elite. The primary distinction here is that the southern political elite only has an internal Superior mentality, totally devoid of an ambitious external like its core-northern counterpart—and the cardinal integrant of this thrust is a more colonial graft of the very affliction in question. And thus this lot is more concerned with swelling the rank and file of its flunkeys than the reduced economic circumstances of southerners; with unctuous following than critical assessments; with peremptory respect for a shallow 'constituted authority' than frank criticisms; with vacuous, populist demagogy than any real ideologically conceived economic or political programme; with the accumulation of wealth and capital than confronting the existential core-northern menace to the socio-political survival of the people in the south. Suffice it to say that the southern political elite shares this affliction in common with its middle-belt counterpart. Evidently, these lot are nowhere near waging a Cold War when their core-northern counterpart is gearing up for a Holocaust.

The Inherent Inferior

There is an epiphenomenon of the Superior affliction which we may call the 'inherent inferior.' It presupposes a reality that whosoever is blighted by the affliction of the Superior is inherently inferior; that they suffer from a rather wretched sub-condition of inadequacy or delusional grandiosity. Although it may be unknown to their consciousness, the 'inherent inferior' is a self-contained derivative of the Superior affliction which is common to the Nigerian political class across the board.

6

DE-NIGERIANIZATION

The precondition to reconditioning the Nigerian contraption is *De-Nigerianization*. The core adversary here is Nigerianization— the very agent of stupefaction perpetuating the Nigerian charade. We must take care to swiftly repudiate Nigerianization for what it is not and avouch it for what it is. There is no prestige of humanistic distinction in Nigeria for Nigerianization, in the same sense that Negritude was as a movement for black consciousness against colonialism and dehumanization. In other words, the Nigerian identity is an identity of deep-dyed oppression, whose very existence is anchored on the persistent exertion of brute force by the state.

For clarity, let us pose a comparison between Negritude, given its peculiar character as a movement for the dignity of the black person, and Nigerianization, for the very reason that it betrays that character. That whilst Negritude was indeed a legitimate impetus against European colonization, Nigerianization is rather an impetus for Nigeria-made recolonization. Whereas the former was about liberation from external monsters, the latter is about subjugation by home-grown monsters. Evidently, as the former was about exuviation—of colonial agitprop, structures and values, the latter is about recultivation of colonial structures and values—by the very stock of home-grown elite Fanon agonized about.

By the same token, De-Nigerianization is about dismantling the plexus of systemic oppression, whilst Nigerianization is about re-imagining and deepening the plexus of systemic oppression. The former caters to progressive humanization but the latter is about *progressive dehumanization*. Nigerianization, therefore, has become the very agent of recolonization against which we must aim our angst, confront and be prepared to tear down.

To understand Nigerianization is to understand

the urgency of De-Nigerianization as a precondition for reconditioning the farcical contraption called Nigeria. Nigerianization is simply *Northernization*. It is northernization in the crude, atavistic sense in which Ahmadu Bello meant it, which Tafawa Balewa proselytized it, which Buhari epitomizes it, which Yerima advocates it, and in fact, the hill on which core-northern imperialists are prepared to die on. It is the imperial ambition that the avarice-driven and cohesion-deficient southern political elite has failed to either discern or vehemently repudiate. The pernicious effect of Nigerianization is the negation of the southern and the middle-beltan person's right to dignity, equality and prosperity or even to exist at all. It enthrones mediocrity and elevates mendacity to statecraft. It ridicules progressive ideas and through the instrumentality of quota system, pulverizes any hope the country has to leap let alone soar. The chief cloven hoof of Nigerianization is not only that it is a mushrooming imperial conspiracy against the freedom and dignity of the ordinary southern and middle-belt person, but also that it is essentially cloaked in the veneer of paternalistic benevolence— our very own pseudo-humanism.

There is a caustic sense in which Nigerianization affirms itself as northernization that bears buttressing.

It is a type of fatalism that induces self-flagellation. For instance, as Nigeria reeled towards the end of Sani Abacha's regime in the late 90s, a Yoruba flunkey of Abacha, Alhaji Alao Arisekola, in one of his blandishments for Abacha's regime's plan to 'civilianize' itself, said: *'the Yoruba people are too clever for their own good. Because they are educated, they think they know everything and so never recognize where their true interests lie... If the Yoruba had any sense in their heads, they would have long realized that it is not the portion of the Yoruba race to rule this nation [Nigeria].'* [18]

Arisekola's vitriol against the Yoruba people should be read not only as a case of a palace clown and his moral turpitude—but also as an indication of ubiquitous vassalage—a blighted state of mind which is a reflection of age-long, multi-ethnic capitulation to northern domination after almost three decades of northern military rule. Across ethnic nationalities in Nigeria today, there are many Arisekolas who engage in self-deprecation and ululate in the puddle of victimhood than fiercely resist the hegemony that is determined to subjugate them and their people for the longest possible time. We must understand, therefore, that when we hear such lofty proclamations

---

18 (Soyinka, 2006)

as national unity, national security, national peace, and other familiar hollow platitudes, we must reject them because they are the very antithesis of those fine ideals and are contrived to stupefy and immobilize the ordinary southern and middle-belt person.

We must reject them, not because they are inherently deplorable, but because our Faustian monsters who glibly glorify them have neither the capacity to actualize them nor the will to actuate the conditions which will conduce to their realization. Nigerianization is the very agent which the political elite wield to daze the ordinary people into believing that the country's concrete reality of oppression and dehumanization are, in fact, liberation and humanization. It stupefies so that the ordinary people are conditioned to see dehumanization as de régle, or at the minimum, be undiscerning to intuit it or too supine to resist it. It stupefies in order to continue to mulct everything from the ordinary people and nothing from the political elite. It stupefies in order to continue to demand application from the ordinary people, even in their dehumanized and reduced circumstances, and demand nothing from the political elite. It stupefies so that the ordinary people are conditioned to see a contradiction as no contradiction at all; so that a fissiparous contrivance is inviolably imposed as unity; paternalism, as righteous; and tokenism, prodigious.

Nigerianization is submission to oppression. Its ultimate goal is a society where people are unable to distinguish between right and wrong; a society where people gleefully embrace mediocrity and destitution. A society where people conflate the political elite—the very enablers of core-northern imperialist siege on the south and middle-belt—as defenders of southern and middle-belt interests with noble intentions. A society where people are victims of mass consumption and miseducation; where people cower in trepidation. In short, Nigerianization is about perpetuating a society where the oppressed are physically and psychologically tortured to surrender their agency under the weight of the violent state piranhas, personified by the police, military and the Department of State Services, DSS. It is the very antipode of civilization, unworthy of collective aspiration.

It satisfies reason hence, that to *de-nigerianize* is to liberate the mind of the ordinary southern and middle-belt person; to grasp oppression and dehumanization in their unvarnished forms; to assert the right to dignity, to disembrace penurious circumstances, to disembrace the rat race of self-application within a bourgeois-controlled society; to disembrace mass consumption and miseducation; to reject tokenism, systemic dysfunction and political bondage as vestiges of colonial inheritance; to assert the right to be free and determine the very essence of one's *being* with the urgency of a people whose backs are against a wall of thorns. To defeat Nigerianization, the ordinary southern and middle-belt person must emerge from that dolorous slumber of fatalism and start tugging at Nigeria's fabric of oppression till it is unmasked and reconditioned.

7

THE IMPERATIVE OF
RECONDITIONING

Reconditioning is an imperative of circumstance, impelled by the purulence of Nigeria's political decay. It emanates from a withered condition, necessitated by a yearning for rectification. It is the banishment of anachronistic degeneration—the extremity of a wretched civilization. It is the realization that what we call Nigeria today cannot sustain itself; that it is foredoomed to crumble under the weight of its own contradictions. 'A civilization that proves incapable of solving the problems it creates,' as Aimé Césaire averred, 'is a decadent civ-

ilization.' Reconditioning is, therefore, a total recon-
struction of a decadent civilization.

Reconditioning ossifies itself as an imperative
which emanates from the cadential manifestations of
state failure: the ordinary person's immiseration and
disaffection, the rampaging of southern and middle-
belt territories by mollycoddled terrorists veneered
as puerile bandits; the bestial incursions dislodging
and decapitating the defenceless in the south and
middle-belt; the mushrooming currency of pillaging
and brigandage—terminating the vulnerable and
entrenching fear among the majority—and in short,
the general anarchy of the status quo under which
Nigeria's material reality is subsumed.

It aligns with reason and objective reality,
therefore, that Nigeria's contemporary reality has
degenerated beyond the sterile, tokenistic gestures of
Restructuring, electoral reforms, constitution review,
Nigerian president 'of Igbo (southeast) extraction[19]',
ethereal intercessions and such other non-measures

---

19 *This idea is either nescient, myopic or purely wicked. The Igbos should
never have to beg for a position which they deserve but have been denied
for several decades. Equity must undergird any genuine and progressive
union, but apparently not Nigeria's union. And even if there were to
emerge an Igbo president in Nigeria as is, such a president will only
be a stooge of the core-north and the bourgeois political elite across the
board.*

that are merely designed to stupefy the mind and delay the inevitable reconditioning. Nigeria's political domain, no matter what it disguises as justice or progressive, is simply a dunghill of retrogrades. The more you dig in the more you sink disreputably. Fela called it 'Egbekegbe.' Reconditioning begins with understanding that it is not just the 'head' of the Nigerian contraption that has fallen to rot; it is the very 'heart' of the contraption that has been infested by the maggots of state failure, core-northern hegemony and imperial ambitions. Reconditioning begins with understanding that Nigeria in its current state can no longer *be,* and the immolation of its concrete existence, as we know it, is of *absolute necessity*.

Before we delineate reconditioning, there is a dialectical opposition that must first be resolved, or at least illustrated, and that is the phenomenon I refer to as secessionist agitation. Contrary to the vituperations of the political elite, secession is the ultimate question to which Nigeria must provide an answer. To understand secession is to understand that it is a motif of two cardinal integrants: on the one hand, is the *absolute secessionist*, and on the other is the *relative secessionist*. Both are allied with secession, but one more consciously than the other. The absolute secessionists are psychologically, ideologically, realistically, and if necessary, violently determined to secede from Nigeria. For this category, we may instance the self-determination groups; Oduduwa Nation and IPOB, who are not a mere creation of the Buhari regime (although he has, in fact, accelerated this contemporary reality) but a concrete culmination of the ordinary southern and middle-belt person's exhaustion with six decades of alienation, dehumanization, destitution, oppression and progressive degeneration. They simply believe in absolute self-determination, with no residual affiliation with the Nigerian contraption. They are the prestos and their credo is simply this: *No one is born united with another and national borders are not engraved in stone—especially when they are carved by colonial butchers—they are creations of the human hand. Even congenitally conjoined twins get separated as soon as surgical alternatives become available so that each may pursue their destiny. The essence of unity is progressive transformation; but when the contrary which is progressive degeneration is the case, that unity becomes purulent—unworthy and incapable of perpetuation. It degenerates to the point of extinction.*

On the other hand, however, the relative secessionists are psychologically jaded with the Nigerian contraption, frustrated with the systemic degeneration, but ideologically quixotic over secession. They are, au fond, trapped between the known evil and the unknown good. They are the faction advocating unity in one breath and lamenting state-backed ethno-nationalist incursions on the other—unable to twig the dialectical opposition between both. They are the civil servants, civil society leaders, trade unionists, media and business moguls, etcetera, etcetera who, though desirous of reconditioning, are cynical about absolute secession—unable to choose freedom over the chains forged against their destinies. They are the lentos and their supposed quandary is simply this: *We know Nigeria is diseased; we know it is atrophying, we know there is elite-conspiracy against the ordinary Nigerian person (or so they say), we know our democracy is illusory—(or anocratic); we know the system is flawed, we know disproportionate violence, venal corruption, immiseration, oppression, dehumanization, destitution, etcetera, etcetera are real in Nigeria, but we are not convinced that absolute secession is the solution.*

To be clear, however, the thrust here is not to emphasize the difference between both faction (even though it is important for dialectical deconstruction), it is simply to posit, that as far as the Nigerian contraption is concerned, *we are all secessionists.* Although, some are more consciously so than others.

There is also an imperative within the imperative of reconditioning: the imperative of convergence or synergy among absolute secessionists. We have seen absolute secessionists in the south but there needs to be *progressive cohesion*—a revolutionary synergy of all absolute secessionists—from all parts of the entire south and the kernel of the middle-belt. It is crucial to expand the revolutionary front lines so that other absolute secessionists, especially those in the middle-belt, would rise from obscurity, shake off the crippling fear and hangover of core-north domination over them, and cohere into the revolutionary wave of absolute secession burgeoning in the south.

Reconditioning as an imperative, in clear terms, is simply this: the forgotten shall be remembered. It entails the following inevitable substratum: First, absolute secession—no reconditioning is visible which is tethered to the Nigerian contraption. Second, a liminal morphological construction—the transitional construction of a congruous national structure that is less a contraption and more a consensus. Simply, the recasting of square pegs in square holes and round pegs, accordingly. Third, organic development—a new approach to development—hard-headed, intentional, innovative, and inclusive.

On absolute secession: there is simply no case stronger, no force mightier and no aspiration greater.

It is the very utility which the Nigerian hegemonic overlords have violently repressed without cessation—most notably reified through the Tiv Agitations, the Isaac Adaka Boro Niger Delta Republic Declaration, the Uncivil War, and subsequently, the Orkar Coup, the Ogoni Agitation, the Oodua Peoples' Congress and other self-determination agitations between then and now which have culminated in the neoteric agitations of IPOB and Yoruba Nation—yet its resurgence remains immutable, and its soul, inviolate. This imperative is irreducible; though there will be attempts by pseudo-revolutionaries or reactionary elements, some of whom will emerge from the very stock against which we must aim our antagonism, some will come from the 'dangerous class' we were warned about—the lumpenproletariat, some of them will be garbed in cassocks and may even declare their version of resistance to vitiate this object. But as we already know, these are the umbilical antitheses of any revolutionary process against which we must eternize vigilance.

They will try, as they have done so far, to foist their double consciousness, as Du Bois aptly described it, on us. They will come as intellectuals who, in their supercilious intellectualism, will attempt to diminish this object with their syllogistic obscurantism—

but we must never let them project their double-consciousness, their own unresolved contradiction of their mental enslavement to the imperious Hausa-Fulani suzerains on us. No ratiocination will suffice, because in actuality there will be none with the force of cogency to inspire what the Algerian writer and political activist, Ferhat Abbas, described in 1936 as a 'patriotic ideal'.

We must emphasize the point here that the decision of the core-north to remain in Nigeria was always a calculated one, a product of disingenuity and imperial intrigue. Like Ahmadu Bello, Tafawa Balewa, before he settled into his imperial role as Nigeria's First post-colonial Prime Minister, vigorously campaigned for a partitioned Nigeria along Northern Muslim and Southern Christian lines. As Balewa threateningly averred '... *If the British quitted Nigeria now at this stage, the Northern people [core-north] would continue their interrupted conquest to the sea.'* [20] When he realized their lives in the core-north would be economically gruelling, among other reasons, without the middle-belt and the south, he tapered off his epideictic on secession and partition. But here we are, six decades later, and the imperial ambition of the

---

20 (Forsyth, 1969)

core-north is becoming more ferociously crystallized, despite having taken a lot from the middle-belt and the south and given almost nothing in return. The ordinary people of the south and middle-belt are now embroiled in a cauldron boiling with state-backed murderers who will stop at nothing to accomplish their eternal imperial ambition. The bourgeois political elite of southern and middle-belt descent have maintained their cardinal thrust of 'profit first,' and the rest of us must choose to either perish with them or live and flourish without them. Absolute secession, therefore, assumes utility.

Absolute secession assumes utility, or ultimate object, for the very reason that Nigeria's unity is a fallacy that exists in name only. It assumes utility for the very reason that self-determination from Nigeria is the Orwellian crimethink from which the ordinary southern and middle-belt person has always been prohibited, but which must nonetheless be fought for. It assumes utility for the very reason that all reforms, all actions, all elite-determined 'national direction' in Nigeria are at best tokenistic concessions, and at worse, tragedies of unimaginable proportions. It is honourable to forfeit one's life in the struggle for absolute secession than to do so in defence of the Nigerian contraption. Absolute secession assumes utility for the very reason that it is the only liberating struggle from decades of the violently enforced 'indissoluble Nigeria' motif. It assumes utility because nothing else can free the ordinary person from the south and middle-belt, ensnared in the core-northern *latifundium* called Nigeria, from unmitigated sanguinary incursions, ethnonationalist venom and undisguised feudal ambitions. It is the imperative of the forgotten, the revolt of the complaisant, the language of the dehumanized, the salvation of the impoverished and the ultimate facilitator of genuine peace and stability. 'People are entitled to freedom and justice,' as the late Jerry Rawlings once said '… let there be no peace if there is no freedom and no justice,' he concluded. Absolute secession, therefore, is simply the immediate object which, as Malcolm X often said, ordinary southerners and middle-beltans must attain by any means necessary. This is no thorn-free path; in fact, it is full of it. But that is exactly the price to pay for true freedom.

On morphological construction: For any structure to enjoy the privilege of indefinite existence, it must be well-founded. The poverty of this rudimentary quality at Nigeria's making is the reason the southerners and middle-beltans must now secede from the misbegotten contraption. In constructing a new nation, there must exist a genuine understanding of equality: the equality of people and nationalities; the equality of justice and opportunities—not 'equal opportunity in darkness,' to borrow the words of Vincent Harding—but equal opportunity in progress. The imperative of morphological construction demands intentionality—an intentional commitment to a nation of consenting and consistent nationalities; a nation of progressive nationalities whose development in today's contraption is encumbered by the core-northern problem and the treacherous elite in the south and middle-belt. This construction is a necessity for conscientious alliances among independent ethnic nationalities, a necessity for collective action and collective prosperity. This construction is neither a reintegration into the Nigerian contraption—nor a recreation of it; it is rather a reorganization outside the Nigerian contraption. It is a concretization of Nigeria's partitioning—the essentializing matrix of absolute secession. The fundamental objective is, again, to remember the forgotten.

The goal is to facilitate such progressive harmony towards true nationalism, true nationhood between the entire south and the kernel of the middle-belt under a popular consensus. This is a *sine qua non* for the absolute evaporation of all vestigial shards of the Nigerian contraption. It would be an opportunity to embrace a new identity, a new dawn for congruous nationalities from the south and middle-belt—the very object which our forebears, Nnamdi Azikiwe, Chukwuemeka Ojukwu, Obafemi Awolowo, J.S. Tarka and others failed to achieve which must now regain animation. It is justice for all those who have been callously dispatched in the Nigerian contraption for their gallantry to confront its absurdity.

More than a century and a half ago, Marx and Engels rightly affirmed that 'every class struggle is a political struggle.' It is therefore crucial, to affirm that this inevitable substratum also entails the dismantling of existing southern and middle-belt power blocs, fattened from the blood and sweat of the ordinary southern and middle-belt proletariat, underclass, plebeian, and generally the ordinary people from these regions. Understanding the class antagonism here is fundamentally significant for any real progress to be made in future or post-secession. All the current political elite, or almost all at least, have mindlessly purloined the resources meant for collective prosperity, arrogated proceeds from all economic resources, destroyed nearly all possibilities for social progress, and must hence be rendered permanently *hors de combat.* Here, these political elites are those who have occupied positions of political authority for four years or more during any of the Four Republics of dehumanization, destitution and oppression in the Nigerian contraption. This is of absolute necessity to obviate a recrudescence of the Nigerian affliction from which we must now flee. This very lot—the political elites—have proven to be the concrete antithesis of a reliable sheet anchor. They must either take their place in history as 'elders' or otherwise embrace indefinite obscurity. Morphological construction is a conscientious abstention from the lizard brain syndrome—*being* for oneself to the detriment of all else—and a concrete embrace of progressive transformation. The ultimate object, again, is this: the forgotten shall be remembered.

On organic development: Organic development is simply a new commitment to socio-economic development. It is an approach to development that spurns the bourgeois capitalists approach to development to build a megacity on mega poverty. The utility here is simply this: until the forgotten ordinary person is remembered and included as a person of dignity in the political and socio-economic chain, progressive transformation is incomplete. Organic development prioritizes collective empowerment, input and justice in all facets of economic, social and political development. It is about equal access, a commensurate reward for labour, and it is an impelling force against cronyism and the personalization of the factors of production. This substratum leaves no one behind; it simply enables each to enhance their ability through the support of fellow citizens and state institutions. It is about Africanizing the development process—focusing on those extraordinary endowments native to our ancestral land. It is about discountenancing the products of mass consumption that reward shiftlessness. To Africanize the development process is to embrace collectivity, inclusivity and progress. It is not atavistic but forward-looking. It is about elevating a brother, a sister, a comrade and a compatriot—not subjugating the *Other*. It is the negation of individualization, the endorsement of collectivism. No puissant civilization erected on a truly equitable foundation suffers systemic degeneration. The goal here is the equipoise of social, economic and political equilibria. Equity is the prerequisite for peace, stability and justice. Organic development must account for all of these.

ACKNOWLEDGEMENTS

This work would have remained a manuscript without the unstinting support of my publisher Abibiman Publishing, ably steered by Onyeka Nwelue. To him, I am unreservedly grateful.

I am also grateful to my editor for his harmonious communion during the editing phase.

Finally, special thanks to David Hundeyin, a kindred spirit of many times.

BIOGRAPHICAL NOTE

Raphael Adebayo is a Nigerian writer whose writings have been published on numerous platforms within Africa and across the globe.

He is an Award-Winning Youth Ambassador whose strivings for the cause of young people and marginalized groups have made a remarkable advocate on socio-political issues in Nigeria and beyond. He is very passionate about social, economic and political developments in Africa. Over the years, he has dedicated many of his literary works to advocating Equality, Justice and Social Change.

He has served on the boards of several youth movements and is also known for his front line roles in distinguished Grassroots Social Movements in Nigeria.

He is a Harvard certified scholar on Religion, Conflict and Peace.